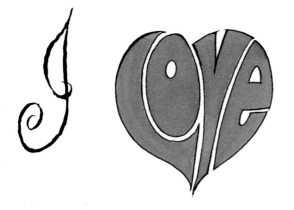

GW00362832

by Roland Fiddy

EXLEY
NEW YORK • WATFORD, UK

Love is the sound of sweet music.

Love lifts you to great heights.

Love tries to impress.

Love is like floating on air.

Love can strike like lightning

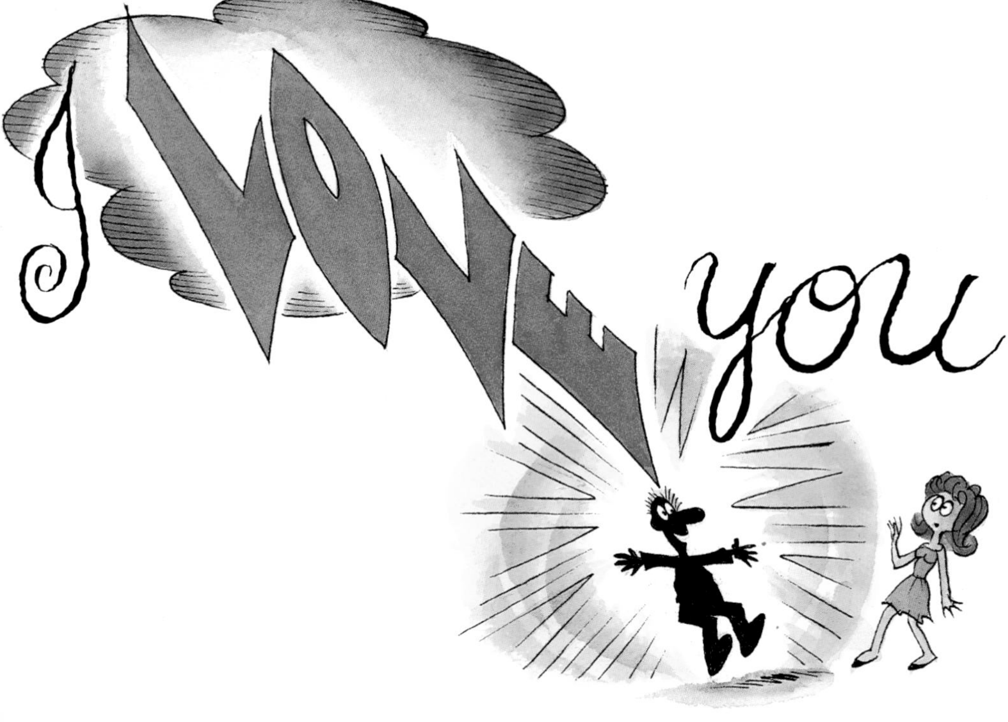
I LOVE you

Love can be a risky business.

Love can sometimes be a rough ride .

Love makes you brave.

Love makes you feel protective.

Love makes all things possible.

Love is an Art .

Love is loyal to the end.

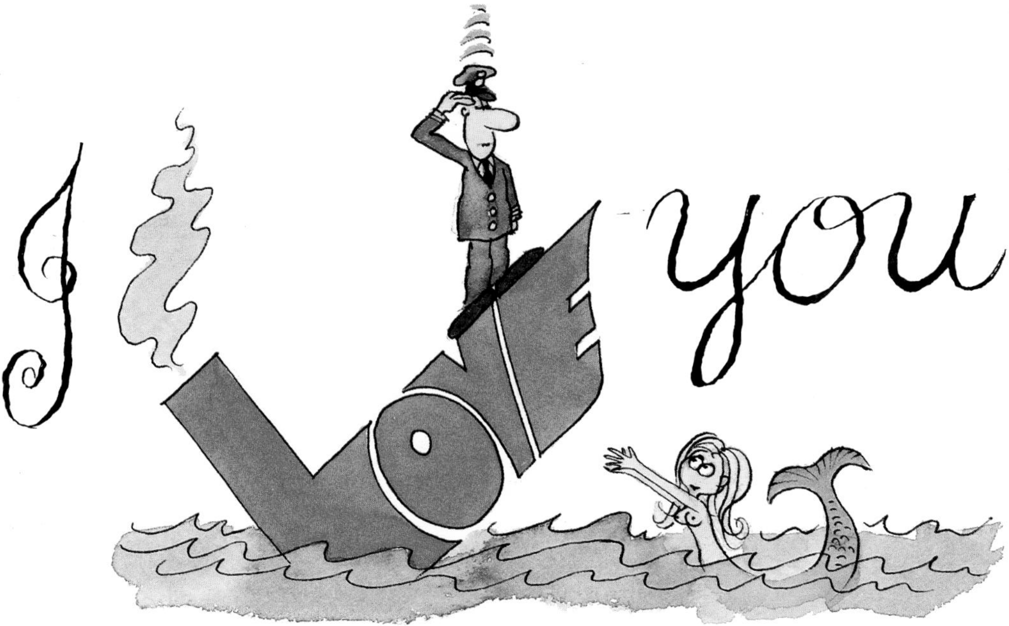
I
LOVE
you